SUNNY DAYS

A First Look

PERCY LEED

Lerner Publications ◆ Minneapolis

Educator Toolbox

Reading books is a great way for kids to express what they're interested in. Before reading this title, ask the reader these questions:

> What do you think this book is about? Look at the cover for clues.

> What do you already know about sunny days?

> What do you want to learn about sunny days?

Let's Read Together

Encourage the reader to use the pictures to understand the text.

Point out when the reader successfully sounds out a word.

Praise the reader for recognizing sight words such as *is* and *the*.

TABLE OF CONTENTS

Sunny Days

It is a sunny day.
The sunshine feels warm.

When it is sunny,
the sky is blue.
It is bright outside.

When it is sunny,
ice cream melts.
Flowers grow.

Why does ice cream melt when it is sunny?

When it is sunny,
skin can burn.

We see our shadows.

When it is sunny, we sit in the shade.

Why do we sit in the shade when it is sunny?

12

We wear sunglasses.

When it is sunny,
we have a picnic.
We go for a walk.

When it is sunny, we run through a sprinkler.

Where do you go swimming?

We go swimming.

When it is sunny,
we play with friends.

A sunny day is fun!

You Connect!

What is something you like about sunny days?

Where do you like to go on a sunny day?

What do you like to do on a sunny day?

STEM Snapshot

Encourage students to think and ask questions like a scientist! Ask the reader:

What is something you learned about sunny days?

What is something you noticed about sunny days in the pictures in this book?

What is something you still don't know about sunny days?

Photo Glossary

picnic

shadows

sprinkler

sunglasses

Learn More

Kenan, Tessa. *Sunny*. Minneapolis: Jump!, 2019.

Murray, Julie. *Summer Weather*. Minneapolis: Abdo, 2022.

Peters, Katie. *The Sun Shines Everywhere*. Minneapolis: Lerner Publications, 2020.

Index

Photo Acknowledgments

The images in this book are used with the permission of: © Olesia Bilkei/Shutterstock Images, p. 4; © sbayram/iStockphoto, pp. 6–7; © Siarhei SHUNTSIKAU/iStockphoto, p. 8; © sergei kochetov/Shutterstock Images, pp. 8–9; © Ground Picture/Shutterstock Images, p. 10; © Martin Barraud/iStockphoto, pp. 11, 23; © Wavebreakmedia/iStockphoto, p. 12; © Robert Kneschke/Shutterstock Images, pp. 13, 23; © NDABCREATIVITY/Adobe Stock, pp. 14–15, 23; © PixelCatchers/iStockphoto, p. 15; © wundervisuals/iStockphoto pp. 16, 23; © SolStock/iStockphoto, p. 17; © Tomwang112/iStockphoto, pp. 18–19; © Image Source/iStockphoto p. 20.

Cover Photograph: © wundervisuals/iStockphoto

Design Elements: © Mighty Media, Inc.

Lerner Publications Company
An imprint of Lerner Publishing Group, Inc.
241 First Avenue North
Minneapolis, MN 55401 USA

For reading levels and more information, look up this title at www.lernerbooks.com.

Main body text set in Mikado a Medium.
Typeface provided by Hannes von Doehren.

Library of Congress Cataloging-in-Publication Data

Names: Leed, Percy, 1968–author.
Title: Sunny days : a first look / Percy Leed.
Description: Minneapolis : Lerner Publications, 2024. | Series: Read about weather. Read for a better world | Includes bibliographical references and index. | Audience: Ages 5–8 | Audience: Grades K–1 | Summary: "Sunny days are the best days. Filled with sunshine, blue skies, and sometimes even ice cream. Colorful photographs and leveled text invite young readers to join in on the fun"—Provided by publisher.
Identifiers: LCCN 2023005570 (print) | LCCN 2023005571 (ebook) | ISBN 9798765608807 (lib. bdg.) | ISBN 9798765616826 (epub)
Subjects: LCSH: Sunshine—Juvenile literature. | Weather—Juvenile literature. | BISAC: JUVENILE NONFICTION / Science & Nature / Earth Sciences / Weather
Classification: LCC QC911.2 .L45 2024 (print) | LCC QC911.2 (ebook) | DDC 551.5/271—dc23/eng20230714

LC record available at https://lccn.loc.gov/2023005570
LC ebook record available at https://lccn.loc.gov/2023005571

Manufactured in the United States of America
1 – CG – 12/15/23